FOUNDATIONS FOR JOY

GOOD NEWS FOR CHRISTIANS

GW00692301

May you know this joy

Jeff

FOUNDATIONS FOR JOY

GOOD NEWS FOR CHRISTIANS

JEFF TRIMINGHAM

RoperPenberthy Publishing Ltd
Horsham, England

Published by RoperPenberthy Publishing Ltd
PO Box 545, Horsham, England RH12 4QW

Text copyright © Jeff Trimingham 2005

First published in Great Britain in 2005
by RoperPenberthy Publishing Ltd

ISBN 1 903905 24 9

Cover design by Angie Moyler

Typeset by Avocet Typeset, Chilton, Aylesbury, Bucks
Printed in the United Kingdom by Cox & Wyman Ltd,
Reading, Berkshire

CONTENTS

DEDICATION

To my dear wife, Doreen, who has loved me for 45 years, borne with me when I was not always living out these truths, often stayed in with our children while I was out teaching them to others, and who rejoices with me in the joy that these truths have brought; thank you!

ACKNOWLEDGEMENTS

Except where otherwise stated, Scripture quotations are taken from the

NEW INTERNATIONAL VERSION Copyright 1978 by New York International Bible Society.

Other quotations are from the

NEW KING JAMES VERSION Copyright 1979, 1980, 1982 by Thomas Nelson, Inc. Used by permission. All rights reserved.

And

THE AMPLIFIED BIBLE, Old Testament copyright 1965, 1987 by the Zondervan Corporation. The Amplified New Testament copyright 1958, 1987 by the Lockman Foundation. Used by permission.

PREFACE

Jesus once said that He wanted His joy to be in us, and our joy to be complete, so if He gets His way with us we will certainly be in for a joyful time! The way by which we enter into that joy is by receiving and embracing the whole of the Gospel and living by it. The word Gospel means "good news", and many Christians view the gospel as being the good news about how to become a born-again believer and receive eternal life, but this is only a small part of the story. I believe that in one respect the gospel can be compared to an iceberg. It is said that only about ten per cent of it shows above the surface, and this is true of the good news. The "how to be saved" bit is only the tip of the iceberg. The other ninety per cent is below the surface, invisible to the natural eye, but once you become a believer, the deeper you go the more good news you find. The Bible states "no eye has seen, no ear has heard, no mind has conceived what God has prepared for those who love him, but God *has revealed it to us by his Spirit*. The Spirit searches all things, even the *deep* things of God" (1 Corinthians 2: 9–10).

It is God's desire that we should grow steadily into a life of love, joy and peace; love for God, the people around us and for ourselves; joy which goes far deeper than happiness, and peace of mind that does not depend on circumstances (or a good insurance policy!). God wants for us a life of fulfilment and purpose and He has made every necessary provision for us to grow into what the Bible calls maturity or completeness. Obviously we cannot attain to maturity overnight but neither does it need to take fifty years as a Christian, in fact it does not automatically come with time at all. It comes through knowledge of God's word and *our response to it.* This does not mean that we must memorise the whole Bible but if we grasp the vital truths about who we are and where we stand in God's estimation this will free us for the rest of our lives from some major hindrances to growth. So come with me below the surface and let's explore the glorious good news that applies to every true believer.

I encourage you to read, study and digest this book one chapter at a time, on your own or with a group of other Christians. At the end of each chapter I have set out some key Bible verses. You will find it very helpful to study, memorise and repeat them until they become built into your thought patterns and attitudes. You may also like to use the suggested prayers as a declaration to God of your intention to live by them. Jesus quoted the Old Testament saying, "Man does not live on bread alone, but on every word that comes from the mouth of God" (Matthew 4: 4), so it is my sincere desire that what follows will set you on the road to growth into a life of fulfilment and joy.

Introduction – Born to Inherit

Imagine an extremely wealthy duke, let us say the "Ninth Duke of Everywhere", who owns a vast estate bringing in huge revenues and who lives in an enormous mansion full of priceless treasures. In course of time he and his wife have a happy event, a baby boy is born. Although this infant is totally unaware of it, he is already heir to a fortune and is destined to become the "Tenth Duke of Everywhere". He did nothing to earn or deserve it, he was simply born to it.

So it is with us as believers; the moment we trusted in Jesus and yielded to His lordship we were born again and we became heirs of God and joint heirs with Christ (Romans 8:17), and we qualified for a beautiful inheritance. The duke's baby son would not inherit until his father died but the good news for us is that Jesus has already died and the inheritance became ours the moment we were born again. Just before Jesus died He shouted in triumph from the cross, "It is accomplished" (John 19:30), meaning that He had already secured and made available to us the many benefits of His sacrifice. He made a will in which He stated, "Peace I leave with you; my peace I give you" (John 14: 27), and He left far more than His peace, as I will explain in more detail in later chapters. He also appointed the Holy Spirit as His Executor, the one commissioned to ensure that the beneficiaries receive what is rightfully theirs. He does this by revealing the meaning of the Scriptures and making them real and relevant to us in our daily life. So we receive this inheritance simply by believing, and we enjoy the blessings of it by living a life "worthy of the calling (we) have received" (Ephesians 4: 1).

Many Christians are robbed of their inheritance, not because Jesus has not made it available to them but because they simply do not realise that it is theirs. Either they don't know because they have never been told, or they don't believe that such blessings could apply to them in this life; they believe that they are reserved for heaven after we die. Let me assure you, from the Scriptures and from my own experience, that the whole of this inheritance is yours to enjoy now if you will believe. If you received a solicitor's letter inviting you to contact them in order to hear something to your advantage you would surely not hesitate to give them a call, so I invite you to examine with me something infinitely better than an earthly will, and it is found in the Bible.

Key Verse

Colossians 1: 12 ... giving thanks to the Father, who has qualified you to share in the inheritance of the saints in the kingdom of light.

1 | THE BIBLE – GOD'S WILL AND TESTAMENT

Thousands of books have been written about the Bible (and here comes another!), and many of them are very helpful, but we must understand that the Bible itself is the supreme authority for our knowledge of God and His will for us. Much of it may seem difficult to understand but we must never dismiss any part of it for that reason. The Bible admits within its own pages that the gospel is foolishness to some people; "to those who are perishing, but to us who are being saved it is the power of God" (1 Corinthians 1: 18). It also states that "all Scripture is God-breathed and is useful for teaching, rebuking, correcting and training in righteousness" (2 Timothy 3:16). It follows from this that our *attitude* to the Bible is all-important; we can choose between treating it as foolishness or as useful, and that choice will affect our destiny.

In our western society we tend to be raised on the assumption that reason is supreme. We wish to reject anything that is not acceptable to our intellect, but if we apply this to the Bible we imply that the Word of God must be subject to our reason, whereas in fact it must be the other way round. This is why I felt it so important to devote this chapter to our attitude to the Bible. Jesus promised that the Holy Spirit (His Executor) would lead us into all truth, so if we are willing to cooperate meekly with Him, He will reveal to us the truth that will set us free to enter into and enjoy that beautiful inheritance.

I have used the word "reveal" deliberately because it

requires something other than a mental grasp of doctrines for us to be led into all truth, and for the truth to set us free. God can reveal truth to our spirit in such a way that we enter into new depths of peace and joy even though we cannot fully understand these matters with our mind. This brings us to a fundamental principle concerning biblical truth. In the area of scientific knowledge we receive facts via our senses, we process them in our minds until we understand, then we believe. As with so many other issues, the Bible way is exactly the opposite; instead of understanding so that we may believe, *we believe so that we may understand*. This is a choice, an act of the will, and when we choose to believe God's Word we are acting in faith, and it is *faith alone* that releases all God's promised blessings to us.

You may be aware that the world is full of different interpretations of the Bible, some of them flatly contradicting each other, but do not let this deter or confuse you. When the apostle John was nearing the end of his gospel he gave us his reason for writing it: he said it was written "that you may believe that Jesus is the Christ, the Son of God, and that by believing you may have life in his name" (John 20: 31). This sums up the purpose of the whole Bible. God's intention for you is that you should experience and enjoy nothing less than His own life inside you, and that life is received by faith, and "faith comes by hearing, and hearing by the Word of God" (Romans 10:17 New King James Version).

As I mentioned earlier, God has made every necessary provision for us to enjoy a life of peace, joy and fulfilment. He has completed His part through what Jesus did, and it now remains for us to believe and receive and live it. Peter wrote, "His divine power has given us everything we need for life and godliness through our knowledge of him who called us by his own glory and goodness", and he goes on to say that, "through these he has given us his very great and precious promises so that through them we may participate in the divine nature" (2 Peter 1: 3–4). The Bible contains about seven thousand promises, and they cover every situation that we are likely to encounter in life, so we are not required to exercise faith for anything that God has not already promised.

The apostle Paul tells us, "no matter how many promises God has made, they are 'Yes' in Christ" (2 Corinthians l: 20). Many of the promises in the Old Testament were conditional on keeping every commandment in the Law of Moses, but Jesus kept every law and fulfilled every condition *on our behalf*, so that is why the promises are now "Yes in Christ", and the only condition required of us is faith. So the whole issue of our growth and progress into that life of love, joy and peace hinges on the written Word of God and the work of the Holy Spirit revealing and applying it to us, and He will do that to the degree that we cooperate with Him by *choosing to believe.*

In the chapters that follow I have not attempted to give a general overview of the teaching of the Bible, but rather to whet your appetite for all the good news: the truth that will set you free. So I encourage you to treat the Bible personally as God's will, in which He sets out what He has bequeathed to you and the conditions for receiving it, and remember, you are an heir of God so you are a beneficiary – happy Bible reading!

Key Verses

2 Timothy 3:16 All Scripture is God-breathed and is useful for teaching, rebuking, correcting and training in righteousness.

Psalm 119:105 Your word is a lamp to my feet and a light to my path.

2 Peter 1:3–4 His divine power has given us everything we need for life and godliness through our knowledge of him

who called us by his own glory and goodness. Through these he has given us his very great and precious promises, so that through them you may participate in the divine nature.

2 Corinthians 1:20 No matter how many promises God has made, they are "Yes" in Christ.

Romans 10:17 Faith comes by hearing, and hearing through the word of God (NKJV).

Prayer

Father, there are many things in the Bible that I do not understand, but I trust your Holy Spirit to reveal them to me, step by step, and I choose to believe, so that I may receive all that you have promised me. Amen.

2 | POSITION *versus* PERFORMANCE

In the chapters that follow you will read some amazing statements from the Bible about yourself, and I can almost guarantee that you will find them incredible, and that word means unbelievable. Take this for example, "we died to sin" (Romans 6:2). You will look at your life, past and present, and then at this Bible statement and probably conclude "no way does this describe me. I am far from being dead to sin, I only wish I was!" If you are like me you will find an enormous gap between what the Bible says about you, on the one hand, and what you see in your own behaviour, on the other. I call this the "credibility gap". We long to close the gap but it just seems out of our reach.

This is a major source of confusion and discouragement among Christians, but we must never call the Word of God incredible. The source of the confusion lies in the fact that we look at what I call our *performance* whereas the Bible is describing our *position*. Let me explain these terms. By our performance I mean our behaviour as compared with the teaching of the Bible, the level of godly living to which we manage to rise. God's standard is very high; for example, He requires us to avoid stealing, lying and criticising others, or even entertaining bad thoughts; we are to love each other, forgive unconditionally any who offend us or hurt us, and even to love our enemies. It must be obvious that you and I fall far short of that standard, even on a good day, and any shortfall from God's standard is sin. So how can the Bible be true when it states that we died to sin?

This is because, as I said earlier, the Bible is describing our *position*. The moment you trusted in Jesus as your Saviour and Lord of your life God placed you in a position in which He regards you as being sinless, not guilty, *as good as Jesus*. That may sound too good to be true but it is the *truth*. You may feel that you don't deserve that position and you would be right, but the wonderful news of the gospel is that when Jesus was crucified God treated Him as we deserved so that when we trust in Him He can *treat us as Jesus deserved*. The Bible states that when we put our faith in Jesus, God credits us with righteousness (Romans 4: 5), which means, put simply, right standing with God. Imagine two bank accounts that record, not money, but righteousness. One belongs to Jesus and the other to you. His statement shows an enormous balance but yours is hopelessly in the red (the Bible sometimes uses the same word for debt and sin). Now at the crucifixion God changed bank statements; all our sins were debited to Jesus and all His righteousness was credited to us, so you are now in the *position* of being debt-free as far as God is concerned.

"That sounds great" you may be thinking, "but the fact remains that I am still continually falling short of God's standard, and that means I am sinning." That may well be a fact, but you must now learn to distinguish between facts and truth. Many do not realise that there is a difference. God's Word is truth (Jesus said so), so Bible truth is eternally true, it always was, it is now and it always will be true and nothing can change it. Many facts, on the other hand, are temporary and subject to change. It used to be a fact that I suffered from angina but since being prayed for, and trusting in God's Word, I don't have it anymore. Bible truth can change the facts but the facts can never change the truth.

Returning, then, to our "credibility gap", you will often

find that the facts about your performance will contradict the truth about your position, and you will be faced with a decision as to which to believe. You will also, I trust, be longing to know how to close the gap; how to live up to the Bible statements about yourself. Here comes another very important principle of Christian living: you don't have to live up to those statements in order to believe them, YOU HAVE TO BELIEVE THEM IN ORDER TO LIVE UP TO THEM. The Bible makes it clear that by our own natural efforts at goodness we can never reach God's standard. That is why He gave Jesus to live up to that level on our behalf and then to die as the punishment for our failure. God's Word says, "if righteousness could be gained through the law (that is living up to God's standard) Christ died for nothing" (Galatians 2:21). So don't expect to live up to those amazing Bible statements about yourself by extra effort and willpower; you will only be disappointed and frustrated. Even the great apostle Paul, who wrote much of the New Testament, frankly admits that "what I want to do I do not do, but what I hate I do", and he goes on to say, "I know that nothing good lives in me, that is, in my sinful nature" (Romans 7: 15,18), so we are in good company!

The important question is "On what grounds do we base our expectation of improvement?" If we focus on our past performance, our "track record", we will expect to fail, so we need a complete change of focus, a different ground of expectation, and this is where God's statements about us come in. We must *choose to believe* them and agree with God's Word because His Word is truth, and remember, truth can change facts. Agreeing with God is such an important subject that I will explain it in more detail in Chapter 5, but for the moment suffice to say that *the more we agree with God's Word the more it becomes a reality in our daily living;* the truth begins to change our "performance facts" and the credibility gap begins to close.

Key Verses

Matthew 4: 4 Man does not live on bread alone, but on every word that comes from the mouth of God.

John 17:17 Your word is truth.

John 8: 31–32 If you hold to my teaching, you are really my disciples. Then you will know the truth, and the truth will set you free.

Prayer

Father, whenever my behaviour or my feelings or my reason conflict with the Bible statements about me, I choose to believe your word, and I trust your Spirit to work in me to close the gap between the two. Amen.

3 | SALVATION – FACT, PROCESS OR HOPE?

Many Christians are plagued with discouragement and confusion in their early days because they find themselves falling into some sin, which leads them to doubt whether they are really saved after all. They have begun to learn about Bible standards of behaviour, and they see other believers *apparently* cruising through life without that problem, and they conclude that "If I were really saved I would never have done that". The credibility gap is just too enormous. In order to avoid this kind of discouragement we need to understand that salvation is in three tenses: past, present and future. The Bible puts it like this: "it is by grace you *have been saved*, through faith" (Ephesians 2: 8). Then, speaking about the message of the cross, it states "to us who are *being saved* it is the power of God" (1 Corinthians 1: 18), yet in Romans 5, verse 9, we read "since we have now been justified by his (Jesus') blood, how much more *shall we be saved* from God's wrath through him". Let me explain.

When you trusted in Jesus as Lord of your life you were saved once and for all from the guilt and penalty of sin. As we saw in the previous chapter, the judgment has already fallen on Jesus, and God would never punish the same sin twice. The sacrifice of Jesus covered not only our past sins but every sin we would ever commit (at the time when Jesus died all our sins were in the future), so we do not become unsaved every time we fall short of God's will. The Bible is very emphatic on this point: "there is now no condemnation for those who are in Christ Jesus, because through Christ Jesus the law of the Spirit of life has set me free from the law of sin and death" (Romans 8:1). I know of no more succinct and clear statement of this truth than this verse from a hymn by Charitie L. de Chenez:

> When Satan tempts me to despair
> And tells me of the guilt within,
> Upward I look, and see Him there
> Who made an end of all my sin.
> Because the sinless Saviour died,
> My sinful soul is counted free;
> For God, the just, is satisfied
> To look on Him and pardon me.

So your place in heaven with Jesus is secure. Having described Himself as the Good Shepherd, Jesus then promised His sheep, "I give them eternal life, and they shall never perish" (John 10:28).

Now let's look at the present tense aspect of salvation. We have already faced the fact that although we are in the position of being dead to sin, yet we are still not free from committing sins. But if we are cooperating with the Holy Spirit at work in us then we are being saved from the power of sin over our lives. We are being progressively set free from sinful habits and attitudes and a sinful lifestyle. The apostle Paul wrote, "offer yourselves to God, as those who **have been** brought from death to life … for sin shall not be your master" (Romans 6:13–14). Before we were saved, sin was our master, although we did not realise it, and living a life that displeased God was accepted as normal, but now we are "under new management". Our new master is Jesus, and as we allow His Spirit in us to change us, we are "being saved".

Finally, we **will be saved** from the very presence and influence of sin, either when we die or when Jesus returns for us, whichever happens first. The Bible promises "the dead in Christ will rise first. After that, we who are still alive and are left will be caught up together with them in the clouds to meet the Lord in the air. And so we will be with the Lord forever" (1 Thessalonians 4:16–17). In that wonderful future state there will be no trace of sin or any of its after-effects.

Another helpful way of understanding these three stages of salvation concerns the three aspects of our own being: spirit, soul and body. You *are* a spirit, you *have* a soul and you *live* in a body. Your spirit is the immortal part of you, which lives on through eternity, either with God in heaven or separated from Him in hell. Your soul is your mind, will and emotions which make up your personality, and your body is the temporary "tent" in which you live on earth.

When you were born again it was your spirit that was made alive. Before that "you were dead in your transgressions and sins" (Ephesians 2:1). So your spirit *has been saved*. It is your soul (mind, will and emotions) that is *being saved* as you allow the Holy Spirit to renew and change it, and it is your body that *will be saved* at the resurrection, when your new body will be "imperishable … raised in glory … raised in power … raised a spiritual body" (1 Corinthians 15: 42–44). It is God's intention that your spirit should rule over your soul, which will then rule your body in a godly way.

To sum up then, you *have been saved* from the guilt and penalty of sin, you *are being saved* from its power over you, and you *will be saved* from its influence and effects. So salvation is a **FACT** *and* a **PROCESS** *and* a **HOPE**.

Key Verses

Romans 8:1 There is now no condemnation for those who are in Christ Jesus, because through Christ Jesus the law of the Spirit of life has set me free from the law of sin and death.

Colossians 1:13 For He has rescued us from the dominion of darkness and brought us into the kingdom of the Son he loves.

John 10: 27–28 My sheep listen to my voice; I know them, and they follow me. I give them eternal life, and they shall never perish.

Prayer

Father, I thank you for giving me eternal life. Help me to show my gratitude by submitting to Your Spirit as He works in me to renew my mind, my will and my emotions. Amen.

4 | *FAITH VERSUS REASON*

In Chapter 1, I mentioned the need to make our reason submit to God's Word if the two appear to conflict, and I will now explain this more fully. At the same time I hope to clear up any possible confusion as to what faith really is. Many people seem to believe that faith is some abstract quality that they must try to raise up within themselves. They look at an older Christian and say, "I wish I had your faith", but this is a misunderstanding. Abraham is portrayed in the Bible as the father of the faithful, and his faith is defined very simply in one statement in Hebrews, chapter 11, verse 11, "He considered Him faithful who had made the promise". Galatians 3: 6 says that "he believed God, and it was credited to him as righteousness", so the essence of Abraham's faith was that he simply believed God and regarded Him as faithful, meaning trustworthy to keep His promises. So, if anyone's faith is real it does not depend on themselves but on *the faithfulness of God.* If you take a specific promise of God in the Bible and consider Him faithful to keep it, then you are exercising the same faith as Abraham, *so don't ever try to measure your own faith against a situation or a problem; measure instead the faithfulness of God* and consider whether He can be relied on to keep His Word.

As you can see, this puts the whole emphasis on what God has already said, and the Bible sums it up this way, "so then, faith comes by hearing, and hearing by the Word of God" (Romans 10:17, NKJV). If we want our faith to grow we need to become more and more aware of God's wonderful promises, and then act on the assumption that He will keep them. The awareness will grow as we study the Bible through reading it and listening to tapes and reading books about it, but, as you may have already discovered, the main hindrance to faith is our mind with its insistence on reason and logic. We need to realise that this rational way of assessing situations is not the only way of looking at them, and it is certainly not the way to receive blessings from God.

The classic Bible definition of faith occurs in Hebrews 11 verse 1: "faith is the substance of things hoped for, the evidence of things not seen" (NKJV). The phrases "hoped for" and "not seen" make it clear that it does not depend on our senses or our reason, and the Bible goes on to say that "the righteous (the believer) will live by his faith" (Habakkuk 2: 4). The converse is that the unrighteous will live by his senses, interpreted by his reason, and he will then be at the mercy of his circumstances! He will receive certain facts via his senses, process them in his mind, and come up with a prediction as to what is likely to happen. Not so the believer; we need a complete reorientation of our outlook, attitudes and interpretation of facts in the light of God's Word. The apostle Paul says, "Do not conform any longer to the pattern of this world, (meaning for example the thought patterns), but be transformed by the renewing of your mind"(Romans 12: 2).

The Bible is full of examples of people who were faced with the choice between reason and faith, and in many cases some enormous consequences hinged on their choice. Let's look at some of these. When Abraham was ninety-nine years old and his wife Sarah was about ninety he was promised that she would become the mother of nations and kings, even though she had been barren all her life and she was now past child-bearing age. His reason must have said "impossible" but, because he believed God, his descendants now number many millions, and God's plan to bless all nations on earth through him is going ahead.

Centuries later, Joshua, as leader of God's people, was faced with the task of capturing the heavily-fortified city of Jericho. The logical battle plan would have been to start building siege ramps, but God's instructions (Joshua chapter 6) were to march around the city blowing trumpets and then, at a given signal, to shout. Imagine the reasonings of a military commander! But when they obeyed, the walls fell down and they took the city. Later still, Gideon found himself in command when the country had just been invaded by an enormous horde of enemy troops. Having mustered an army of a mere 32,000 he was then told by God to send home all but 300, and they were armed with trumpets and torches! To human reason this could not possibly make any sense, in fact it must have seemed suicidal, but when they chose faith in God's Word rather than reason, God completely routed the enemy army.

The miracles of Jesus illustrate this principle many times over, but let me suggest just one. (You may find it helpful to read John chapter 11, verses 1 to 44 at this point.) Jesus got a message that His friend Lazarus was seriously ill, so reason demanded an urgent response, yet Jesus stayed where He was two more days. He said, "This sickness will not end in death. No, it is for God's glory so that God's Son may be glorified through it" (v.4). He then set off for Bethany when He knew that Lazarus was already dead (when reason said that it was too late). By the time Jesus arrived, Lazarus had been dead and buried for four days and the natural (reasoned) reaction of both of his sisters was "if you had been here my brother would not have died". The final affront to reason came when Jesus said to open the tomb, and Martha protested, "by this time there is a bad odour, for he has been there four days". The response of Jesus was, "Did I not tell you that *if you believed, you would see the glory of God?*" He then brought Lazarus out of the tomb by His *word of faith* and He told the others to *action their faith* by taking off the grave clothes and setting Lazarus free.

So then, the "good news" in this chapter is that we do not need to try to screw up more faith from within ourselves but rather to remember that "He who promised is faithful"(Hebrews 10: 23). Someone may ask, "Are you advocating that we fly in the face of reason?" I would say that if reason flies in the face of the Word of God then *yes*, we need to stay focused on God's promise for that situation, irrespective of the circumstances or symptoms. One subtle way in which our reason may still try to hinder is by causing us to try to work out *how* God could bring this about, but the "how" is God's concern, not ours. As Jesus said to a man whose young daughter had just died, "Don't be afraid, just believe".

Key Verses

Hebrews 11: 1 Faith is the substance of things hoped for, the evidence of things not seen.

Romans 10: 17 Faith comes by hearing, and hearing by the word of God.

Hebrews 10: 23 He who promised is faithful.

Prayer

Father, please help me to recognise when my reason is opposing or questioning your Word. I choose to believe your Word every time. Amen.

5 | AGREEING WITH GOD

In Chapter 2, I stressed the importance of agreeing with God regarding the Bible statements about ourselves, and because this applies to all God's Word about any and every subject, I promised to explain in more detail.

The Bible says, "it is with your heart that you believe and are justified, and it is with your mouth that you confess and are saved"(Romans 10:10). We tend to think of the word "confess" as meaning to own up to God or someone else about something we have done wrong, but it has a far wider significance than that. The Greek word translated as "confess" literally means "to say the same thing", so when we confess sins to God we do not inform Him of anything that He did not know about, but we are calling that behaviour by the same name as He calls it. We are agreeing with Him that it was sin and, here comes some more good news, when we do that we can also *agree with God that it is forgiven.*

Returning to our text in Romans, the second part of that verse could be translated, "it is with your mouth that you confess *into salvation".* You may remember that in Chapter 3, I explained about salvation being in three tenses: past, present and future. In the first instance this verse refers to the time when we trusted in Jesus as our Saviour and confessed (agreed) that He should be our Lord. At that moment we became saved (past tense) from the guilt and penalty of sin; but there is also a continuous sense. We can be continually confessing ourselves further and further into that "present tense salvation" so that our mind, will and emotions become "more saved", that is, more free from the habit and power of sin and more in line with the mind and will of God. We do this by agreeing with God about everything He says, and in particular, everything He says about us.

However, there is more: the "key verse" says that it is with your mouth that you confess into salvation. It is not just a matter of mental assent to God's Word but we are to *say* the same things as He says. It is extremely important that we learn to live by this principle. We need to make a conscious decision to agree with God's assessment of ourselves, of other people, and of our circumstances; and we will become more and more aware of His assessments and opinions as we read and study the Bible. Then we can choose to agree with Him and to *tell Him* so by speaking out the relevant part of His Word.

I have already mentioned Joshua and his capture of Jericho, but before he and the Israelites crossed the river to approach that city, God gave him some general instructions that were His recipe for success. Referring to the small part of the Bible that had so far been written, God said, "Do not let this book of the Law depart from your mouth, meditate on it day and night, so that you may be careful to do all that is written in it", and this instruction was then followed by a promise, "then you will be prosperous and successful" (Joshua 1:8). Notice that God did not tell him not to let it depart from his mind, but from his mouth, and the Hebrew word for meditate in that text actually means to mutter! *God knows that there is beneficial, faith–building power in His Word when we speak it out as an expression of our agreement.*

This is sometimes called making a positive confession, but it is all too easy to make a negative one without realising it. Suppose you are faced with a really difficult situation or problem and you cannot see any way through it. A negative confession would be, "I'll never solve this problem, I just can't cope", but a positive confession might be, "I can do everything through him who gives me strength" (Philippians 4:13). Please note that this is not merely a difference between pessimism and optimism, because *what we say is likely to influence the outcome.* In Mark Chapter 11 Jesus strongly emphasised the power of our words. He had just caused a fig tree to wither by the words He spoke to it, and He then said to His disciples, "whoever says to this mountain, 'Be removed and be cast into the sea', and does not doubt in his heart, but believes that those things he says will be done, *he will have whatever he says*" (verse 23, NKJV, italics mine). Jesus was stating the principle that we get what we speak for, either positive or negative, either spoken in faith or unbelief.

The Bible contains many illustrations of this principle at work in the lives of various people, but I can think of no more graphic example than that found in the book of Numbers, chapters 13 and 14, and it would be helpful to read that story at this point. The people of Israel stood on the threshold of the land that God had promised them, and Moses sent in twelve men to spy out the land and report back. The spies all saw the same situation but they produced two entirely different reports with completely conflicting recommendations. Ten of them said "We can't attack those people, they are stronger than we are ... we seemed like grasshoppers in our own eyes and we looked the same to them". On the other hand, Caleb, along with Joshua, said, "We can certainly do it". The people in general sided with the majority view and they spoke a dreadful thing over themselves: "If only we had died in Egypt! Or in this desert!" (negative confession!). God said "I will do the very things I heard you say: in this desert your bodies will fall", and the final outcome was that every one of those people got what they spoke for. Those who said, "We'll never make it" never made it, and the two who said, "We can certainly do it" finally entered into the land of God's promise.

The book of Revelation speaks, in Chapter 12, about "our brothers", and says that, "They overcame him (Satan) by the blood of the Lamb (Jesus) and by *the word of their testimony*". The blood of the Lamb is God's part (and has already been completed), but we have a choice as to what kind of testimony or confession we make, and that will decide the degree to which we "overcome", or how far we *confess into salvation.* So be encouraged! You can grow in faith and in joy and peace as you make a habit of *agreeing with God.*

Key Verse

Romans 10:10 It is with your heart that you believe and are justified, and it is with your mouth that you confess and are saved.

Prayer

Father, please help me to grow in my awareness and understanding of your Word as it applies to my life. I choose to agree with your promises and statements about every situation. Amen.

6 | WE DIED TO SIN

This phrase in Romans Chapter 6 is one of those amazing statements about us that we may find difficult to believe but, as I said in Chapter 2, it refers to our position rather than our performance, but we need to know how this truth is meant to affect the way we live. If it is merely a point of doctrine without any obvious application then it is not good news. I would suggest that you read the whole of Romans Chapter 6 at this point, and if you have access to the Amplified Bible all the better.

The good news is that, when we turned from a life independent of God and submitted to Jesus as Lord, our old self died, even though we may not have felt anything, and our spirit came alive; we were born again. This was not something that we achieved, it was accomplished by Jesus. "He himself bore our sins in his body on the tree, so that we might die to sins and live for righteousness" (1 Peter 2: 24). So it is not a question of wondering whether what we did has really worked; what Jesus did has definitely worked!

Our old self was totally incapable of pleasing God because it was distorted and twisted, just as a bent ruler would be unable to guide a pencil in a straight line. Living independently of God was regarded as normal, and pleasing ourselves was "only natural", but in reality this is the essence of sin, and "the wages of sin is death" (Romans 6: 23). To put it another way, if we work for sin all our lives the pension it pays is death. (This refers not merely to physical death, which is separation from the body, but also to spiritual death, which is separation from God forever.) In this "natural" state we were *bound to sin*, meaning that we were tied to it and unable to separate ourselves from it, and that it was inevitable that we would go on sinning. That was the bad news but look at the good news: "we know that our old (unrenewed) self was nailed to the cross with Him in order that (our) body, (which is the instrument) of sin, might be made ineffective and inactive for evil, that we might no longer be slaves of sin" (Romans 6: 6 Amplified Bible). A dead body is completely inactive in regard to sin! As for when this took place, it happened at the moment when we surrendered to Jesus. The statement that our old self was nailed to the cross means that, in effect, our death to sin was back-dated to His crucifixion, so this was one of the many benefits included by Jesus when He cried from the cross, "It is accomplished".

If you reflect on your life since you believed, you may be discouraged to find that you are still capable of sinning, but can you now do it with a clear conscience? If you now feel bad about doing those things which previously didn't trouble you then be encouraged. This shows that you have already died to sin, in the sense that you have lost the love of sinning and, more good news, whenever you do fall short of God's will for you there is an instant remedy: "If we confess our sins, he is faithful and just and will forgive us our sins and purify us from all unrighteousness" (1 John 1:9). It used to puzzle me as to how God could be *just* in forgiving me when I deserved to be punished but, as we saw in Chapter 3, since He has already punished Jesus for that sin He would be unjust if He judged the same sin twice.

Take a look at the first two verses of Romans Chapter 8: "Therefore, there is now no condemnation for those who are in Christ Jesus, because through Christ Jesus the law of the Spirit of life set me free from the law of sin and death". The word "law" in this text does not mean a rule or a piece of legislation but rather a governing principle, like the laws of science which tell us what to expect from a certain cause. The "law" of sin states that death must follow, but the "law of the Spirit" says that eternal life will result from trusting in Jesus, and because this new law overrides the old one we are completely exempt from its effects.

How then should we respond to all this good news? In Chapter 2 we saw that we must *believe* these amazing statements about ourselves *in order to live up to them*, and in this context the key lies in verse 11 of Romans Chapter 6: "count yourselves dead to sin but alive to God in Christ Jesus". This verse is not encouraging us to engage in wishful thinking, far from it. The Greek word literally means "to count, to occupy oneself with reckonings or calculations", so we are dealing with facts and truths not wishes. We are to assume and take it for granted that we do not have to sin; we may not be incapable of sinning but we are *capable of not sinning* because we have a "new self". We are not only dead to sin but we are alive to God and, according to Ephesians 4: 24, our new self has been "created according to God, in true righteousness and holiness" (NKJV). This refers to our spirit which was *created like God* when we were born again. So we are to put off our old self and put on the new, in the knowledge that our new self is already righteous and holy, and when we focus on that new self we really can live to please God. He has "rescued us from the dominion of darkness and brought us into the kingdom of the Son He loves" (Colossians 1:13), and when we live day by day in that kingdom then pleasing God "goes with the territory". So let's have no nostalgic visits to our old haunts and habits please!

On a practical level, we need to shift our whole emphasis off sin and onto Jesus. It is a mistake to begin the day by thinking of particular sins to avoid; you have already focused on them! *Do not expect to sin*. Rather, let us concentrate on Jesus who doesn't have a sin problem and *who lives in us*. More of that in the next chapter.

Key Verses

Romans 6:6 We know that our old self was crucified with him (Jesus).

Romans 6:2 We died to sin; how can we live in it any longer?

Romans 8:2 Through Christ Jesus the law of the Spirit of life set me free from the law of sin and death.

Romans 6:11 Count yourselves dead to sin but alive to God in Christ Jesus.

Prayer

Father, I thank you that my old self has died and that I am free from compulsion to sin. I choose to believe this truth and, with the help of Jesus in me, I expect to live a life that pleases you. Amen.

7 | JESUS IN YOU

If you have ever struggled with the "daunting task" of trying to live a godly life, if you have tried and failed and felt discouraged, then here comes a wonderful piece of good news. Yes, God does require a high standard of behaviour, as do some other religions but, unlike any of the others, God offers to empower us to maintain that standard by *living in us*. Of course, we are free to reject His offer but Jesus warned us that "apart from me you can do nothing" (John 15: 5).

Years after Jesus returned to heaven He promised, through the Apostle John, "Here I am! I stand at the door and knock. If anyone hears my voice and opens the door, I will come in and eat with him, and he with me" (Revelation 3: 20). The door to which He refers is the entrance into our lives, and the truth is that at the moment when we surrendered our lives to Him, He came in. That simple promise contains what the Apostle Paul calls "the mystery of the gospel". He writes about "the mystery that has been kept hidden for ages and generations, but is now disclosed to the saints (that's us!). To them God has chosen to make known among the Gentiles the glorious riches of this mystery, which is *Christ in you, the hope of glory*" (Colossians 1: 26,27).

The phrase "the hope of glory" has more than one meaning. It can be taken to mean that Christ in us is our hope of reaching glory in the form of heaven when we leave this life. He is indeed the guarantee of our eternal destiny but, in the present context, it is helpful to realise that Jesus in us is our hope (and our only hope!) of bringing glory to God by the way we live. So here is the secret, the "mystery", of how to live a godly life; *"I have been crucified with Christ and I no longer live, but Christ lives in me.* The life I live in the body, I live by faith in the Son of God, who loved me and gave himself for me" (Galatians 2: 20).

As with all these wonderful truths in the Bible, we are tempted to check this out against our senses – can I feel Jesus in me? Or we test it against our performance – am I behaving as if Jesus lives in me? The answer to both questions is likely to be "no", but does this mean that this Bible statement does not refer to us? No! Once again we have a choice between doubting, and thereby missing the benefits of this truth, or *believing in order to experience the reality.* When we view our failures and shortcomings we need to look to Jesus in us as our source of godliness. He alone is *the ground of our expectation of improvement.* When Paul despairs of his own efforts at pleasing God he cries, "Who will rescue me from this body of death?" Then he answers his own question: "Thanks be to God – through Jesus Christ our Lord!" (Romans 7: 24,25).

In his second letter to Christians, Peter states the same truth: "His divine power has given us everything we need for life and godliness through our knowledge of him who called us by his own glory and goodness" (2 Peter 1:3). He is saying that through Jesus living in us we have got what it takes to meet every situation in a godly way, and, to the degree that we believe it and act on the assumption that this is true, we really will meet those situations and treat those people in a godly way. Jesus has all the virtues that are needed to cope with every challenge, every disappointment, every setback, every offence and every crisis that we will ever meet, and every habit or attitude that has been letting us down, and, *because He lives in us we can draw on those virtues.* Paul writes, "I can do everything through him who gives me strength" (Philippians 4:13). Another way of translating this would be, *"I am strong for everything in Christ who empowers me".* We are strong when we draw on His virtues.

Of all the Bible statements about us, I find that the most amazing one, and the hardest to believe, is found in 1 Corinthians 2:16: "we have the mind of Christ". If I play back some of the thoughts and attitudes that I find in my mind I am strongly tempted to disbelieve this Scripture, but if I do disbelieve it I am hindering Jesus in me. Remember, He can only work through the faith that we give Him because He does not overrule our free will. Let's face it, this statement cannot possibly make sense until we realise and acknowledge that "Christ lives in me", but as we choose to believe it we will allow Jesus, by His Spirit, to progressively change our mind and its attitudes to bring them more into line with His.

How then does this truth of Christ in us become a reality? How do we draw on His virtues? The key lies in our *expectation.* The word Christ means "the anointed one", and carries the sense of being commissioned and empowered for a particular purpose. In His case that purpose was to carry out and fulfil in every detail the will of God, and since He lives in us, we too have received not only the commission but also the empowering. As we believe *and speak* our agreement with this wonderful truth we can *expect to live a godly life.*

Key Verses

Galatians 3:20 I have been crucified with Christ and I no longer live, but Christ lives in me.

2 Peter 1:3 His divine power has given us everything we need for life and godliness.

Philippians 4:13 I can do everything through him who gives me strength.

Colossians 1:27 Christ in you, the hope of glory.

Prayer

Father, I thank you for giving Jesus to live in me. I commit myself to act on the assumption that this is true and, through Him, I expect to meet every situation in a godly way. Amen.

8 | SEATED WITH CHRIST

"God has raised us up with Christ and seated us with him in the heavenly realms in Christ Jesus" (Ephesians 2: 6). This verse sets out clearly our position, which we looked at in Chapter 2. If we are born again, then regardless of the progress in godly living that we have made so far, or the lack of it, our *position* is one of total, unconditional acceptance by God because of what Jesus achieved, and because His achievement was credited to us at the moment when we yielded to Him. We are regarded by God as completely righteous, meaning in right standing with Him. "God made him (Jesus) who had no sin to be sin for us, so that in him we might become the righteousness of God" (2 Corinthians 5: 21). An understanding of this Scripture should bring a tremendous sense of relief, because it means that any efforts on our part to make ourselves more acceptable to God are *completely superfluous because we have been made righteous.* Therefore let us look a little more deeply into the Bible verse with which we began.

In order to avoid confusion it is important to understand the meaning of the phrase "heavenly realms". If we thought that this meant heaven, being the place where God lives, then we would tend to project this statement into the future time when we leave this earthly life, and we would thereby miss the liberating effect that it is meant to have on our present life. Actually the same phrase occurs in Chapter 6 of Ephesians to describe the area of warfare against the spiritual forces of evil, so it certainly doesn't mean heaven. I think it is helpful to understand the "heavenly realms" as being *the sphere of spiritual reality or spiritual truth* (remembering that truth supersedes facts), so it is a spiritual reality that we are seated with Christ.

The second point to note is that it was God who placed us in that position; "*God* has raised us up with Christ". We did not attain this position by any effort or merit of our own, nor could we ever do so. It was entirely by God's grace, His unmerited favour towards us. Therefore it follows that we do not keep or maintain this high position by any other means. We trust solely in the unfailing, unconditional love of God. Please also notice that God *has* seated us with Christ. This statement is in the past tense, so it is not a promise for the future, nor a mere invitation to rise to that position, but a clear statement of what God has already done; it is included in what Jesus meant when He cried from the cross, "It is finished", or accomplished or completed, (John 19: 30). As with our death to sin, our positioning with Christ in the heavenly realms was back-dated to the crucifixion, when we trusted in Him.

We come now to the significance of the word "seated". Referring to Jesus, Hebrews 10:12 says "when this priest had offered for all time one sacrifice for sins, he sat down at the right hand of God". As this sacrifice was "for all time" He sat down to rest for all time because He had finished work for all time. The fourth chapter of Hebrews refers back to the creation of the world, and to the fact that on the seventh day (called the Sabbath) God rested from His work, and then, in verses 9 to 11, the Scripture says "There remains, then, a Sabbath-rest for the people of God; for anyone who enters God's rest also *rests from his own work*, just as God did from his. Let us, therefore, make every effort to enter that rest". (The last phrase certainly does not imply self-effort; a more accurate translation would be "let us be eager to enter that rest".)

So we are urged by God to rest from our own work and to be eager to enter into His rest. Jesus made the same kind of invitation one day when He said "Come to me, all you who are weary and burdened, and I will give you rest" (Matthew 11: 28). What, then, is the work from which we are invited to rest? Jesus was not offering to do the ploughing and reaping for the people of His day: He meant rest from the "work" of trying to please God and find acceptance with Him by keeping rules and regulations through self-effort. As we have already seen, this is completely impossible and any such effort only leads to failure, frustration and condemnation. The good news conveyed by this wonderful truth is that when God raised us up and seated us with Christ *He lifted us to the same level of acceptance as Jesus.* This may sound too good to be true but, as we shall see in the next chapter, God wishes to treat us as being on an equal footing with His Son.

To sum up, then, the truth that we have been seated with Christ in the heavenly realms means that we can rest and cease from all striving to find favour with God. This exalted position or status of being totally accepted and embraced by our heavenly Father is *not our destination but our starting point.* As we respond in gratitude to this amazing grace we will naturally want to live up to our status, and, because Jesus lives in and through us, we should expect to do so!

Key Verses

Ephesians 2: 6 God has raised us up with Christ and seated us with him in the heavenly realms in Christ Jesus.

2 Corinthians 5: 21 God made him who had no sin to be sin for us, so that in him we might become the righteousness of God.

Prayer

Father, I thank you for lifting me to this place of acceptance and rest. Please show me more and more clearly the significance of this truth, so that in my daily life I may respond with gratitude and loving obedience. Amen.

9 | *JOINT HEIRS WITH CHRIST*

"To all who received him (Jesus), to those who believed in his name, he gave the right to become children of God" (John 1:12).

There is a sense in which every human being is God's offspring, in that He created us all, but, following the rebellion of our ancestor Adam, we became estranged and lost from Him, and we would have stayed that way had not God sent His Son to reconcile us to Himself. The world in general has rejected the One who created it, but, as the verse quoted above shows, those who "receive" Jesus are accepted into God's immediate family. I say immediate family because God has no grandchildren; we are not accepted on the strength of our parents' behaviour or even their faith. We are either born again or we have no relationship with God at all, but those who receive Jesus as Lord are given all the privileges of sons and daughters. When the Apostle John wrote his first letter to Christians he seemed to be thrilled all over again; he says, "How great is the love the Father has lavished on us, that we should be called children of God! And that is what we are!" (1 John 3:1).

The cause for joy gets even better: in the introduction I wrote about the newborn son of an imaginary duke being the heir to his father's estate. This status would only be afforded to the firstborn son, but when we are "born from above", whether male or female, we are treated as being

God's firstborn son, *His heir.* "You received the Spirit of sonship. And by him we cry 'Abba, Father'. The Spirit himself testifies with our spirit that we are God's children. Now if we are children, then we are heirs – heirs of God and co-heirs with Christ" (Romans 8: 15–17). As I hinted in the last chapter, this really does mean that God treats us as being on a level with Jesus as regards our position, our status, and our relationship with Him. *God loves you every bit as much as He loves His Son.*

A statement like this may well seem hard to believe, especially for those who have had a raw deal in life, perhaps from their own family members, but please remember, *we must choose to believe Bible truth* regardless of how we feel. The whole gospel is summed up in one verse: "God so loved the world that he gave his one and only Son, that whoever believes in him shall not perish but have eternal life" (John 3:16). If you substitute your name for "the world", that shows how much God loves you. At the height of His agony on the cross Jesus cried out, "My God, my God, why have you forsaken me?" (Matthew 27: 46). On that dreadful day God had to choose either to forsake you and me or to forsake His own Son, and look whom He chose! That is an indication of the value that God puts on our lives, and the length to which He went in order to reconcile us to Himself. We have been adopted into God's family, the family of the King, and that makes us royal family! "So now you are no longer a slave, but a son; and since you are a son, God has made you also an heir" (Galatians 4: 7).

This exalted status naturally carries with it great responsibilities and wonderful privileges. We are responsible to behave at all times in a way that brings credit and honour to our Father's name, but, as we saw in chapter 7, we are not left to achieve this in our own strength. God has given us His Holy Spirit, the Spirit of Jesus, to live that life in and through us, and the more we cooperate with Him the more honour we will bring to our Father. As for the privileges, these take many forms but I believe they can be summed up in the one, glorious, all-encompassing truth that we have been brought into an intimate relationship with God. The Creator of the universe is our loving Father, and each of us is His dearly loved son and heir. We can approach Him at any time of day or night, knowing that this relationship will never change, and that we can always count on His *undivided attention*. No human being can give his undivided attention to many people all at once but God is God and He can!

As this privileged relationship was conferred on us entirely by God's grace, this leaves no cause for pride or arrogance, but, on the other hand, there is, in the life of the believer, no room for low self-esteem either. The Bible says "Do not conform any longer to the pattern of this world, but be transformed by the renewing of your mind" (Romans 12: 2). This means that we are to abandon the attitudes of this world and have our minds renewed to take on the attitudes of God, and *that includes His attitude to us*. Regardless of our background, intelligence, education (or lack of it), social status or anything else, you and I are the objects of God's intense love. No matter how many people may have rejected you in some way, the Lord of heaven and earth has personally called you and adopted you into a position of unconditional acceptance as His cherished son or daughter. In a class-conscious society people may describe someone as being "well-connected", meaning that they are related to someone of great wealth, power and influence, but we, as believers, are directly related to the "King of kings and Lord of lords", and you can't be better connected than that!

I believe that the need to belong is inherent in every human being, and when this need is not met the resulting feeling of rejection or loneliness is a major ill in our society, but when we receive Jesus as our Saviour and Lord we can begin to enjoy a close relationship with a

Father whose love never wavers or varies according to our behaviour. He treats us as being on a level with His sinless Son, and as we believe this, and live our lives in gratitude for this amazing grace, we enjoy more and more of the privileges, and our relationship grows ever closer.

Key Verses

John 1:12 To all who received him (Jesus), to those who believed in his name, he gave the right to become children of God.

Romans 8:16–17 The Spirit himself testifies with our spirit that we are God's children. Now if we are children, then we are heirs – heirs of God and co-heirs with Christ .

1 John 3:1 How great is the love the Father has lavished on us, that we should be called children of God! And that is what we are!

Prayer

Father, I thank you for adopting me into your family and treating me as a joint heir with Jesus. Please help me to grow in my understanding and appreciation of this, so that I may live in a way that brings credit to your name. Amen.

10 | HIDDEN WITH CHRIST

When we were born again we became what the Bible calls "in Christ". There is a whole wealth of meaning in this phrase and it is not possible in this book to do justice to every aspect, but my purpose in this present chapter is to show how safe we are, in this life and the next.

"In Christ" we are now one with Him spiritually; His death was our death to sin, His life is our life, and His future is our future. The Bible states, "If we have been united with him like this in his death, we will certainly also be united with him in his resurrection" (Romans 6: 5), and "When Christ, *who is your life*, appears, then you also will appear with him in glory" (Colossians 3: 4). So our destiny is now inextricably bound up with the destiny of Jesus. Referring back to "Agreeing with God" in Chapter 5, this is a truth that we need to believe, receive, repeat and settle in our minds, so that, whatever our present circumstances, we have that certain hope for the future.

Jesus referred to His followers as His sheep and to Himself as the Good Shepherd, and He said "My sheep listen to my voice; I know them, and they follow me. I give them eternal life, and they shall never perish; no one can snatch them out of my hand" (John 10: 27,28). So our eternal destiny is assured, but what about those present circumstances to which I just referred? What about the "here and now" which always seems more real than our eternal future? We need assurance about our safety in this present life with all its problems, uncertainties and threats, so here it comes! God has given us very many promises on this subject throughout the Bible, but let's focus on one or two key verses in particular: "You died, and your life is now hidden with Christ in God" (Colossians 3: 3). As an illustration of this truth, let your Bible represent God; take two bookmarks, one to represent Jesus and the other yourself, then place them together in the middle of the Bible and close it. As the bookmarks are safely hidden together in the Bible, so your life is hidden together with Christ in God. I can think of no safer environment than that, and the Bible is emphatic that this is an accomplished fact, not a promise for the future.

God has provided a protective covering for every one of His children in this present life, and this is beautifully described in Psalm 91, in statements like these: "He who dwells in the shelter of the Most High will rest in the shadow of the Almighty" (verse 1); "He will cover you with his feathers, and under his wings you will find refuge" (verse 4); "If you make the Most High your dwelling – even the Lord, who is my refuge – then no harm will befall you" (verses 9,10). It will be helpful to read and digest the whole psalm and to treat it as God's personal promises to you. As with all God's blessings, however, they are only received and enjoyed by faith. As the psalm says, it is the person who "dwells" in the shelter of the Most High that will rest in His shadow. This means adopting a *lifestyle* of trusting whatever God says in His Word, and not giving way to doubts and fears. This is a *choice* we need to make. We have the free will to step out of God's protective covering by wilfully disobeying Him or *by not trusting His Word*. Over one hundred times in the Bible God has commanded us to "fear not", *so there is no place in the life of a Christian for any kind of fear or worry.* Of course these emotions will arise from time to time, but we need not give way to them or entertain them when we remind ourselves of the promises that God has made. If, in any situation, we become worried or fearful we imply either that God cannot cope, or that He doesn't care, or both; and when viewed like that we must admit that this would be an insult to Him.

I cannot overemphasise the truth that we have a free will to choose to declare God's protection promises over ourselves and to *act on the assumption that He will always keep them.* If I may borrow a phrase from space fiction, this is like "activating the defence shield" of God's power by using our faith in His Word. When we trust God in this way then *our safety becomes His responsibility.* So why not make a quality decision to actively put on God's protective covering on a daily basis by agreeing with His promises, and if we find ourselves slipping into doubts or anxieties then we apologise to Him, receive His forgiveness and quickly get back under cover!

Key Verses

Colossians 3:3 You died, and your life is hidden with Christ in God.

John 10: 27,28 My sheep listen to my voice; I give them eternal life, and they shall never perish.

Psalm 91: 9,10 If you make the Most High your dwelling – even the Lord who is my refuge – then no harm will befall you.

Prayer

Father, I thank you that I am eternally united with Jesus in His death, His life, and His future. Because my life is hidden with Him in you, I am completely free from anxiety or fear in this life and the next. Thank you for Your peace. Amen.

11 | GOD'S ATTITUDE TO YOU

Jesus once said, "with God all things are possible" (Matthew 19: 26). Most Christians are convinced that this statement it true, but, when it comes to making requests to God in prayer, many people do not ask with full assurance of faith because they are not sure of God's *willingness* to bless them in a particular way. They may be hindered by thoughts of not deserving something, or that God is not interested in such small matters. This shows a lack of understanding of God's underlying attitude to us, and we may miss out on much that He wants to do for us, and in us, unless we are clear on this issue. A man once came up to Jesus, in an advanced state of leprosy, and said, "if you are willing you can make me clean". The reply of Jesus was instant and clear: "I am willing, be clean" (Luke 5:12,13). In a sense, the whole Bible is a revelation of God's attitude to us, but I have chosen some sample passages to illustrate this.

When God had rescued His people from slavery in Egypt He gave them His laws, His "rules for happy living". He then promised that, if they obeyed, He would grant them the most wonderful lifestyle that anyone could wish for. This is described in detail in passages such as Leviticus 26: 3–13, Deuteronomy 7:12–15, and Deuteronomy 28:1–14. Take a few minutes to study these, and picture the kind of life they would enjoy. It included complete peace and security, safety from enemies and wild animals, freedom from every disease (Deut. 7:15), "abundant prosperity" (Deut. 28:11), and a sense of identity in belonging to God. Sadly, the people of Israel never fully entered into this idyllic lifestyle because they did not obey God's laws, but He did not make these amazing promises knowing full well that He would be safe from having to fulfil them. *He wanted them to obey so that He could lavish those blessings on them,* and He would have kept every promise He made. This was God's attitude to His people, and, because He does not change, *His attitude to you and me is just the same.*

Centuries later, even when God's people were in persistent disobedience and rebellion, He spoke to them through the prophet Isaiah saying, "the Lord longs to be gracious to you; he rises to show you compassion" (Isaiah 30:18). Picture your Heavenly Father sitting on His throne, scanning the earth, looking for someone to whom He can be gracious, and when He finds someone who gives Him the opportunity, He rises to greet them and bless them. This attitude of God is beautifully illustrated in the story, told by Jesus, of the lost son, in Luke Chapter 15. During the whole time that the "prodigal son" was away bringing disgrace on himself, his father was no doubt scanning the distant road, hoping to catch sight of him, "longing to be gracious" to him, and when he did come into view his father ran to embrace him without any questions or condemnation, and showered gifts on him.

Those blessings described in the Old Testament were conditional on obedience, but the heart of the gospel, or good news, in the New Testament, is that Jesus obeyed all the laws on our behalf, and God then credited us with that obedience. Jesus went even further; He took on Himself all the curses described in Deuteronomy Chapter 28 so that we might never suffer them for our disobedience: "Christ redeemed us from the curse of the law by becoming a curse for us" (Galatians 3:13). Every true believer is therefore in a position to receive *all* the blessings that the Bible records: "For no matter how many promises God has made, they are 'yes' in Christ. And so through him the 'Amen' is spoken by us to the glory of God" (2 Corinthians 1: 20). The word amen means "truly", so the only condition required of us is faith, that is, simply taking God at His Word, agreeing with Him (saying "truly"), and expecting to receive what He promised.

This is the very point at which so many Christians fail to receive. All the blessings promised in the Bible are God's desire for us but they are not conveyed automatically. We can block them by our lack of faith. For example, although God had promised His people that wonderful life in the land of Canaan, all but two of the mature adults died in the desert without ever seeing it because "the message they heard was of no value to them, *because those who heard did not combine it with faith*" (Hebrews 4: 2). Similarly, when Jesus was healing sickness and disease on every side, He came to His home town but "*could* not do any miracles there, except lay his hands on a few sick people and heal them. And he was amazed at their lack of faith" (Mark 6: 5,6). So we see that we can prevent God from satisfying His own desire to bless us in every way, by our unbelief, *and that unbelief includes doubting His willingness*.

God's willingness to bless us is summed up in a very brief statement that occurs twice in the fourth chapter of John's first letter: "GOD IS LOVE" (1 John 4: 8,16). John does not say that God does love, or has love, but that He *is* love. Because that is God's nature and He is unchanging, this means that *He cannot help loving us* – even if He wanted to – and *He cannot stop loving us*, regardless of how we behave. Please take time to allow this truth to saturate your mind and heart, because *this is the ultimate answer to every doubt regarding His willingness.* When we add to that His almighty power – "with God all things are possible" – and His absolute faithfulness to His own Word, then, with that kind of assurance, we can give God the faith that He needs to work with, and our loving Heavenly Father is free to satisfy His desire on His children.

Key Verses

Isaiah 30:18 The Lord longs to be gracious to you; he rises to show you compassion.

2 Corinthians 1: 20 No matter how many promises God has made, they are "Yes" in Christ.

1 John 4: 8 God is love.

Prayer

Heavenly Father, thank you for loving me so much. I would not want to frustrate you in any way by my unbelief, so please help me to trust ever more fully in your love and your promises, so that you are free to fulfil in me all your desires and purposes. Amen.

12 | *HEALTH AND PROVISION*

"Beloved, I pray that you may prosper in all things and be in health, just as your soul prospers" (3 John 2: NKJV).

We have established, in Chapter 1, that "all scripture is God-breathed" (1 Timothy 3:16), so whatever a Bible author wrote to believers in the first century, God is saying to us. The text quoted above shows God's wishes concerning our health and material provision. We should never be in any doubt about this, so, when approaching God on matters like these, which are covered by Bible promises, we need *never* pray, "if it is Your will". Look again at the reply of Jesus to the leper, quoted in the previous chapter: "I am willing, be clean". He has made His will very clear!

Let us look at health first. In the last chapter I referred to Deuteronomy Chapter 7, verse 15, where God promised through Moses, "The Lord will keep you free from every disease". That solemn promise shows God's intention towards all His children. At that time the fulfilment was conditional on obedience, and, in the latter part of Chapter 28 of that book, God warned that the awful consequences of disobedience would include sickness and disease; but part of the glorious good news of the Gospel is that God sent Jesus to fulfil the conditions for us, and then to suffer those dreadful consequences of our disobedience. Isaiah prophesied this over seven hundred years before it happened, when he wrote, "surely he took up our infirmities (meaning sickness, weakness, pain) and carried our sorrows (meaning pain)" (Isaiah 53: 4).

When Matthew described an incident in which Jesus healed every sick person present, he said that it was fulfilling this prophecy (Matthew 8: 17). Peter also took up the theme when he quoted the next verse of Isaiah; "(Jesus) himself bore our sins in his body on the tree, so that we might die to sins and live for righteousness; by his wounds you have been healed" (1 Peter 2: 24). The Bible is quite emphatic at this point. The word translated "healed" occurs 28 times in the New Testament and in all but one case it means actual bodily or mental healing. The verb is also in the past, or "completed" tense, so this Scripture is saying that Jesus has *already accomplished* all that is necessary for our healing. When He suffered on the cross He "took up" our sickness and "carried" our pain, so that we would not need to take up or carry them, and He became our permanent remedy.

So God has not only made His wishes clear, but He has also made full provision for us to live in health. He has already done His part, and now it remains for us to "confess" His Word with our mouths and receive His promises by faith. The Bible contains many more promises on this subject, and the world contains many thousands of people who can testify to God's faithfulness in keeping them, when they approached Him in simple faith, so I encourage you to be "simple" in your faith!

We turn now to the subject of God's provision for our material needs. The verse I quoted at the head of this chapter shows His wishes in this area. To the people of Israel He had promised, "The Lord will grant you abundant prosperity" (Deuteronomy 28: 11). Under that Old Covenant this was conditional on their obedience and, in particular, they were to honour God by giving Him a tenth of their income: "Honour the Lord with your wealth, with the firstfruits of all your crops; then your barns will be filled to overflowing, and your vats will brim over with new wine" (Proverbs 3: 9,10). Many years later, when they were persistently ignoring the command, God appealed to them: "'Bring the whole tithe into the storehouse, that there may be food in my house. Test me in this', says the Lord Almighty, 'and see if I will not throw open the floodgates of heaven and pour out so much blessing that you will not have room enough for it'" (Malachi 3: 10). Notice the lavish promises that accompanied God's requirement.

In the New Testament it becomes clear that the whole subject of financial provision works on the principle of sowing and reaping, and the money we give to God is regarded as seed being sown into His kingdom. Jesus taught, "Give, and it will be given to you. A good measure, pressed down, shaken together and running over, will be poured into your lap. For with the measure you use, it will be measured to you" (Luke 6: 38). Following the farming analogy, common sense tells us that if we sow a small amount of seed we will reap a small harvest, and Paul spells this out in his second letter to the Corinthians: "Remember this: Whoever sows sparingly will also reap sparingly, and whoever sows generously will also reap generously" (2 Corinthians 9: 6). In that same chapter, Paul goes on to assure us that, "God is able to make *all* grace abound to you, so that in *all* things at *all* times, having *all* that you need, you will abound in every good work" (v.8). "You will be made rich in every way so that you can be generous on every occasion" (v.11).

Back in the Old Testament God's people were warned, "But remember the Lord your God, for it is he who gives you the ability to produce wealth, and so confirms his covenant" (Deuteronomy 8: 18), and from the New Testament passages above, it is clear that God's reason for granting the wealth is "so that you can be generous on every occasion". I believe that we can summarise the whole subject by saying that God wants us to be in financial freedom, freedom from lack, and freedom from the fear of lack; "So do not worry, saying, 'What shall we eat?' or 'What shall we drink?' or 'What shall we wear?' For the pagans run after all these things, and your heavenly Father knows that you need them. But seek first his kingdom and his righteousness, and all these things will be given to you as well" (Matthew 6: 31–33). To those who are "sowing" in faith into God's kingdom comes this absolute guarantee: "My God will meet all your needs according to his glorious riches in Christ Jesus" (Philippians 4: 19). These lines from an old hymn seem to crystallize the whole subject:

> Make but His service your delight;
> Your wants shall be His care.

Key Verses

3 John 2 Beloved, I pray that you may prosper in all things and be in health, just as your soul prospers (NKJV).

1 Peter 2: 24 He himself bore our sins in his body on the tree, so that we might die to sins and live for righteousness; by his wounds you have been healed.

Proverbs 3: 9,10 Honour the Lord with your wealth, with the firstfruits of all your crops; then your barns will be filled to overflowing, and your vats will brim over with new wine.

Luke 6: 38 Give, and it will be given to you. A good measure, pressed down, shaken together and running over, will be poured into your lap.

2 Corinthians 9: 8 God is able to make all grace abound to you, so that in all things at all times, having all that you need, you will abound in every good work.

Philippians 4: 19 My God will meet all your needs according to his glorious riches in Christ Jesus.

Prayer

Father, I thank you for your loving provision, through Jesus, for my health and material well-being. Please help me to receive these blessings by simple faith in your promises, and by giving freely as an expression of my gratitude. Amen.

13 | COMPREHENSIVE COVER

At this point I wish to draw together some strands from previous chapters in order to emphasise a truth which certainly is a major "foundation for joy". We have already seen that the Bible is God's will and testament, in which He reveals what He has bequeathed to us as the beneficiaries, but the Greek word translated "testament" also means "covenant", and the more deeply we understand this word, the greater will be our peace and joy.

Normally a covenant is a binding agreement between two parties, setting out conditions which each undertakes to fulfil, but God, in His grace, has made one-sided, unconditional covenants with us. To Abraham He promised descendants as numerous as the stars, and that they would possess the land where he was a wandering stranger, and that *through him all nations on earth would be blessed.* When Abraham asked God "How can I know that I will gain possession of it?" God replied with an awesome ceremony in which He instructed him to cut several animals in two and lay the pieces opposite each other, and then God caused a smoking firepot and a blazing torch to pass between the pieces (see Genesis, Chapter 15). In the Old Testament one of the words often used to denote "making" a covenant literally means *to cut,* and, in the culture of his day, the significance of this would not have been lost on Abraham. It was as if God was saying, "If ever I break this covenant may I be as one of these animals". He had "cut" a covenant with Abraham.

God had bound Himself, by this oath, to bless the

descendants of Abraham, and the New Testament makes it clear that, "If you belong to Christ, then you are Abraham's seed, and *heirs according to the promise*" (Galatians 3: 29), so that includes us, and God laid down no conditions for this promise. As if this were not a wonderful prospect in itself, God then established His New Covenant, in which He promised to put His own Spirit, His very life, into the hearts of those who would believe, and this covenant was sealed, not with the blood of animals, but *with the blood of His own sinless Son.* Again, far from imposing any preconditions on us, "God demonstrated his own love for us in this: While we were still sinners, Christ died for us" (Romans 5: 8). The collective promises of God are described in the Bible as His covenant of peace, and He promises *"Though the mountains be shaken and the hills be removed, yet my unfailing love for you will not be shaken nor my covenant of peace be removed"* (Isaiah 54: 10).

Insurance companies like to promise us peace of mind – at a price, but God's all-embracing promises constitute a far superior "policy". They provide not only life cover but *eternal life cover* from the moment we are born again. Many product guarantees exclude misuse or neglect, and it goes without saying that we cannot expect to enjoy the fullness of God's blessings if we misuse our bodies or neglect the "Maker's instructions" in the Bible; but, with that proviso, there are no exclusions; every aspect of our life is covered (see Chapters 10 and 12, for example), and every claim, made by faith in His promises, will be met. Some policies include "excesses", voluntary or otherwise, requiring us to pay part of the cost of any claim, but the only contribution that God requires from us is, as always, simple faith in His Word. Perhaps the best, and the most humbling aspect of God's insurance policy is the premium. It is a single payment which is absolutely beyond our means, and *it has been pain in full on our behalf! Jesus died to secure our "cover".*

This whole subject of covenant is beautifully illustrated

in an incident in the life of King David, as recorded in the Second Book of Samuel. Years earlier, when Saul was still king, his son Jonathan had befriended David and had made a covenant with him. As a symbol of this commitment he had given David his prince's robe, his tunic, and even his sword and bow and his weapons' belt. Thus they had sworn to be ever loyal to each other and to defend each other if necessary. Subsequently this put Jonathan in a very difficult position because his father became embittered against David and repeatedly tried to kill him, but he kept his promise. Sadly, Jonathan was later killed in battle along with his father, and David became king over Israel. Jonathan had a little boy called Mephibosheth, and when the tragic news reached the family, his nurse snatched him up and fled in fear for his life, and in the panic, Mephibosheth fell, or was dropped, and became crippled for life. When he grew up he lived in obscurity, even though he was the grandson of the late king.

A covenant always included the descendants of the two parties, and when David became established and secure in his kingdom he still longed to honour his covenant with Jonathan (now read on, in 2 Samuel, Chapter 9!). What David did for Mephibosheth has close parallels with what God did for us. He sought him out in order to bring him out of obscurity and bless him, just as "the Son of Man came to seek and to save what was lost" (Luke 19: 10). He banished fear and promised kindness, just as God has done to us throughout the Bible. He restored to Mephibosheth all his grandfather's estate, in other words, he received back his rightful inheritance which had been lost through his grandfather's disobedience. In the same way, God has restored to us the inheritance that we lost through Adam's disobedience (see my Introduction – "Born to inherit"). Finally, David decreed that Mephibosheth should always eat at the king's table, like one of the king's sons, just as we have been made joint heirs with Christ (see Chapter 9 – "Sons of God"). So Mephibosheth received all this wonderful treatment because of a binding covenant that David had made with his father.

The ninth chapter of 2 Samuel ends with the words "and he was crippled in both feet". The sad irony of the story is that Mephibosheth need never have been crippled or living in obscurity *if only he and his family had known about the covenant.*

In Chapter 11, on God's attitude to us, we saw that all the promises of God are "yes" in Christ, but the clear implication of His covenant with us goes far beyond His mere willingness to bless us; *if He ever broke a single promise He would be denying His own nature and dishonouring the blood of His Son.* He is therefore bound, by His own solemn covenant, to bless those who come to Him in submission and faith. This life of peace, security and joy, in this world and the next, was secured for us, once and for all, by the death and resurrection of Jesus. Please take time to reflect on this awesome truth. Once we have committed our lives to Jesus, God takes full responsibility for our total well-being, and there can be no room for doubt or anxiety when we understand and appreciate God's "comprehensive cover".

Key Verses

John 10: 10 I came that they may have and enjoy life, and have it in abundance – to the full, till it overflows (Amplified Bible).

Isaiah 54: 10 Though the mountains be shaken and the hills be removed, yet my unfailing love for you will not be shaken nor my covenant of peace be removed.

Prayer

Father, I thank you that my whole life is covered by your covenant of love and peace. May your Holy Spirit guard my heart from any doubts or fears. I choose to trust in your unfailing love. Amen.

14 | POWER FOR SERVICE

In Chapter 7 we saw that Jesus is the power we need for godly living – "the hope of glory". Living a Christian lifestyle by New Testament standards is not difficult, it is downright impossible – in our own strength, but as we believe and acknowledge the presence of Jesus in us we can draw on His virtue and goodness. However, the power that God offers us goes beyond the mere ability to maintain a godly standard of behaviour. Jesus said, "anyone who has faith in me will do what I have been doing. He will do even greater things than these, because I am going to the Father" (John 14: 12). It is that kind of power that I will explain in this chapter.

After Jesus rose from the dead He told His followers to go into all the world and spread the good news of all that He had achieved for them, but then He warned them, "stay in the city until you have been clothed with power from on high" (Luke 24: 49); "do not leave Jerusalem, but wait for the gift my Father promised ... in a few days you will be baptised in the Holy Spirit ... you will receive power when the Holy Spirit comes on you" (Acts 1: 4,5,8). Even though those men had spent three years being trained by Jesus, hearing His teaching and witnessing His miracles, they were not yet ready to fulfil His commission until they were *supernaturally empowered for service.*

Not many days after Jesus spoke those words His promise was fulfilled, not only in His chosen close disciples but also in a group of about 120 believers, who were all "filled with the Holy Spirit". It is this event, described in detail in Acts, Chapter 2, that launched the believers into a supernatural lifestyle, enabling them to start doing what Jesus had been doing, as He had promised. The change in the disciples was dramatic. Before being filled with the Spirit they were meeting behind locked doors "for fear of the Jews" (John 20: 19), but, within minutes of receiving that gift, Peter, who had even denied knowing Jesus, stood up in front of thousands of those same people and fearlessly told them the truth about Him. At the risk of his own life he told them, "God has made this Jesus, whom you crucified, both Lord and Christ" (Acts 2: 36). Having called on them to repent and be baptised, he then made a very significant statement: "You will receive the gift of the Holy Spirit. The promise is for you and your children and for all who are far off – for all whom the Lord our God will call" (Acts 2: 38,39).

This supernatural empowering by the Holy Spirit was not reserved for the original twelve apostles, nor for modern day ministers or missionaries, but is promised to all believers. Shortly after receiving this gift, Peter and John instantly healed a forty-year-old man who had been crippled from birth, and these kinds of miracles, and even more amazing ones, are happening on a massive scale all over the world today. The twelfth chapter of 1 Corinthians lists nine different supernatural gifts available to believers, but it is not the purpose of this book to explain them in detail. There are various books on this subject, which you may find helpful when your appetite is whetted! However, I will describe some of the benefits, on a personal level, of being baptised in the Holy Spirit.

In my own case, and that of many others, one of the most significant results was a new insight and understanding of the Bible and its relevance and application to my daily life. Items of Bible knowledge which had previously seemed like separate pieces of a jigsaw puzzle suddenly "came together" to reveal thrilling aspects of the truth. (Without this gift I would have been unable to write this book, as I have had no formal training in theology!) I experienced a new hunger for more knowledge and understanding of the Bible, which became an exciting book which I enjoyed reading. The Holy Spirit also brought me into a much more intimate relationship with God as my Father and Jesus as my Saviour. I had absolute assurance of my salvation and my eternal destiny, and *God wants this for every believer*. A deep, inexplicable joy is a normal by-product of this experience, and this leads to a desire to share it with others. The ability to speak in tongues is also a normal accompaniment of the baptism in the Holy Spirit. This is a very precious gift which enables our spirit to communicate directly with God without having to rely on our mind knowing what to say. It may be used both in personal praise and worship, and also in praying for people and situations for which God wants us to pray. The Bible states, "I would like every one of you to speak in tongues" (1 Corinthians 14: 5), and when we use this gift regularly it is a constant assurance that we are gifted by God in a supernatural way.

This assurance of supernatural gifting is something which we will need on many occasions as we come up against seemingly impossible situations and insurmountable problems. We may be required sometimes to undertake tasks for which, in the natural, we are simply not adequate, but throughout the Bible a clear promise emerges. It takes many forms and is expressed in various ways, but the reassuring message is the same. In Chapter 4, I referred to a man called Gideon. He was nervous and totally lacking in self-confidence, yet he was told by God to lead the whole nation in battle against their oppressors. God's word to him was, "Go in the strength you have and save Israel out of Midian's hand. Am I not sending you?" (Judges 6: 14). He was to go in the strength that he thought he did not have, but which God would supply. This, then, is the promise that I mentioned above: *God never commis-*

sions us to any task without empowering us to perform it.

Jesus called this empowering *"the* promise of the Father" (Luke 24: 49 NKJV). Peter declared that it is "for all whom the Lord our God will call" (Acts 2: 39), and Jesus specifically encouraged us to ask for it (see key verse below). So the implication is clear: in whatever way God calls us to serve Him, He promises us power for service.

Key Verses

Acts 1: 8 You will receive power when the Holy Spirit comes on you.

Acts 2: 39 The promise is for you and your children and for all who are far off – for all whom the Lord our God will call.

Luke 11: 13 If you then, though you are evil, know how to give good gifts to your children, how much more will your Father in heaven give the Holy Spirit to those who ask him!

Prayer

Father, I trust in your faithfulness to all your promises, and I thank you for the promise of your supernatural power. I acknowledge my need, and I ask you now to grant me this gift. By faith I receive the ability to fulfil all your purposes for my life. Amen.

15 | GOD'S GOAL FOR YOU

It is a good thing to have objectives or goals in life because they provide us with motivation, and without a target we have no idea whether we are hitting or missing. It is clear from the Bible that God has very definite goals for every believer, and I would like to draw your attention to some of these. When the apostle Paul was writing letters to various churches he revealed how he prayed for them, and because all Scripture is "God-breathed", we can be assured that Paul's desire for the early Christians is God's desire for us. However, I must stress at the outset that these are *not* some kind of attainment targets which we either pass or fail to achieve. I present these to you as a great source of encouragement, because God possesses both the will and the power to enable us to reach these goals, *if we cooperate with Him*. So let's take a look at God's goal for you.

In Paul's prayers there is a very strong emphasis on knowledge, but he is not referring to mere head knowledge. For those in Ephesus he prays for the Spirit of wisdom and revelation (Ephesians 1: 17–19). Wisdom may be defined as the right use of knowledge, and the establishing of practical, workable principles to live by; and revelation comes when the Word of God becomes real and relevant to us personally, and we gain a clear perception of truth and how to apply it. Paul prays this so that they (and we) may *know* God better. In particular, God wants us to know the hope to which He has called us, in other words, the goal which He expects to achieve in and through us. He also wants us to know the enormous power that He has made available on our behalf, such as the power that raised Jesus from the dead. What a life of confidence we can live when we realise, or really *know* this!

For the Christians in Philippi, Paul prays, "that your love may abound more and more in knowledge and depth of insight, so that you may be able to discern what is best and may be pure and blameless until the day of Christ, filled with the fruit of righteousness that comes through Jesus Christ – to the glory and praise of God" (Philippians 1: 9–11). This shows that there is a very strong link between knowledge and love. As our knowledge of God grows we will love Him all the more deeply, and as our love grows He will release to us more knowledge and depth of insight. This, in turn, will enable us to "discern what is best" as we make choices through life; which brings us back again to wisdom.

From Paul's prayer for the believers in Colosse (Colossians 1: 9–12), it is clear that God wants us to be filled with the knowledge of His will through all spiritual wisdom and understanding. Many people struggle over the issue of finding God's will, and many books have been written on the subject, but we need to remember that the source of all this knowledge, insight, wisdom and revelation is twofold; the Bible and the Holy Spirit, and both are available to us at any time. Spiritual wisdom and knowledge do not depend on intelligence or education; we all have equal access to them through this two-fold source, so we can be assured that this goal for us is attainable.

Paul records another of his prayers in the third chapter of Ephesians (verses 16–19): "I pray that out of his glorious riches he may strengthen you with power through his Spirit in your inner being, *so that Christ may dwell in your hearts through faith*." This is not to deny that Jesus came to live in us from the time when we truly believed (see Chapter 7), but it is God's desire that we should grow in our *consciousness* of this truth, so that it governs our thinking and behaviour and lifestyle. Paul then goes on to pray, "that you, being rooted and established in love, may have power, together with all the saints, to grasp how wide and long and high and deep is the love of Christ, and to know this love that surpasses knowledge." Knowledge of the love of God is the ultimate source of the peace and joy that He wants for us, and please notice that this knowledge surpasses knowledge! How can this be? Simply because spiritual knowledge surpasses the natural kind, and is the only kind by which we can know God.

The last clause of this prayer is perhaps the most amazing: *"that you may be filled to the measure of all the fullness of God"*. We may be tempted to think that Paul has now drifted above the realms of realism, but he repeats the same prospect in the next chapter. In discussing the ministry of apostles, prophets, evangelists, pastors and teachers, he states that, the objective is that "we all reach unity in the faith and in the knowledge of the Son of God and become mature, *attaining to the whole measure of the fullness of Christ"* (Ephesians 4: 13), and he says that the goal of his own ministry is *"that we may present everyone perfect in Christ"* (Colossians 1: 28). The word "perfect", here, does not mean "sinless perfection" but "completeness", not lacking any of the virtues that God imparts by His Spirit.

This, then, is the amazing goal that God has for us: that we should be filled with the fullness of Christ, with all His virtues. Paul sums it up in his letter to the Christians in Rome, and this time his words are not in the form of a prayer but rather a statement of God's intention: *"For those God foreknew he also predestined to be conformed to the likeness of his Son"* (Romans 8: 29). God's goal is that we should become like Jesus, in this life, not merely when we get to heaven. I am well aware that, for many, this may seem a hopelessly tall order, far beyond their expectations, but let me encourage you. I mentioned, at the beginning of this chapter, that God possesses both the will and the power to enable us to reach these goals. Jesus is described as "the author *and finisher* of our faith (Hebrews 12: 2 NKJV), and this is where our confidence must be placed. Paul writes, "being confident of this, *that he who began a good work in you will carry it on to completion until the day of Christ Jesus*" (Philippians 1: 6).

I also mentioned earlier that the attainment of these goals requires our cooperation; it certainly does not happen automatically, so how can we cooperate? I believe that first and foremost we must begin with a positive attitude, in which we not only set out to achieve God's goals, but that we *believe that they are attainable* through the Holy Spirit living in us. We can then work with the Spirit by devoting ourselves to reading, meditating and digesting the Bible, and by spending quality time with God in prayer, discussing all our affairs with Him and telling Him of our admiration of Him. We also stimulate our growth by meeting with other Christians for worship, teaching and fellowship, always with our focus on Jesus. By these means we can help the Holy Spirit in His work of changing us into the likeness of Jesus. So be encouraged! Jesus is the goal and the means by which we reach it.

Key Verses

Romans 8: 29 For those God foreknew he also predestined to be conformed to the likeness of his Son.

Hebrews 12: 2 Let us fix our eyes on Jesus, the author and perfecter of our faith.

Philippians 1: 6 He who began a good work in you will carry it on to completion until the day of Christ Jesus.

Prayer

Father, I thank you that you have chosen such a destiny for me, that I should become like Jesus. I welcome your plans for my life, and I set myself in agreement with them. Please help me to know you better as I commit myself to prayer and studying your Word. Amen.

16 | PRAYER AND PEACE

In the Introduction I referred to the will of Jesus, in which He bequeathed to us His peace, and in Chapter 13 we saw that God describes His all-embracing covenant with His children as "my covenant of peace" (Isaiah 54: 10), so I would not want to conclude this book without setting out the secret of that peace.

At the beginning of John Chapter 14 Jesus said, "Do not let your hearts be troubled". I am aware that this is easier said than done; many Christians have a real struggle with this, and similar Scriptures, because their mind tells them that they cannot help being troubled or anxious when certain circumstances arise; it is only natural to worry. Yes, it is "only natural", but we are no longer living in the "only natural" and we are not bound by its conditions and dictates any more: "If anyone is in Christ, he is a new creation; the old has gone, the new has come!" (2 Corinthians 5: 17). The words of Jesus, quoted above, are not a suggestion but a command, so it follows that God has made available to us the ability to obey it. When anxious thoughts attack our minds we are told not to allow them to stay, but how do we stop them? I imagine that you have already discovered that simply trying to fight them off does not work; they will return again and again as our mind reviews the situation.

The secret lies not in trying to suppress our emotions but in *replacing our anxious thoughts with the words of God.* As believers we will certainly wish to pray in times of crisis or trouble, but if we pray in fear we are not praying in faith, and without faith we cannot receive the help that we need. Psalm 55: 22 says, "Cast your cares on the Lord and he will sustain you", so there needs to be a conscious "casting", and we can only do this if we are confident that God will be there to catch them! However, as we learn more of God's promises and His general attitude to us (see Chapter 11), this will give us the confidence that we need, and the greater our knowledge the greater will be our confidence.

One of the many promises on this subject is found in Isaiah 26: 3: "You will keep him in perfect peace, whose mind is stayed on you" (NKJV). The word "stayed" in this verse means sustained or supported, and here lies the secret of a life of unbroken peace. God is very gracious in answering our "emergency calls" to Him, but if we wish to enjoy that *lifestyle of peace* which Jesus left to us, we will need to *programme our mind with God's promises*, so that we have an internal supply on which we can draw when threats arise. When our minds are "stayed" on God in this way, then we can know His perfect peace.

It really is possible to enjoy a kind of peace that does not depend on our circumstances being agreeable. When Paul was writing to the Philippian church he said, "Do not be anxious about anything, but in everything, by prayer and petition, with thanksgiving, present your requests to God" (Philippians 4: 6). Like Jesus, he is saying that we must *make a decision* not to allow our natural emotions to rule our mind, but rather, we are to turn the issue over to God and make our requests to Him, in full assurance that He knows all about our situation, and that He cares, and is well able to cope. Please note that we are to do this *with thanksgiving*. However threatening or negative a situation may appear, there are always grounds for thanking God, and a positive decision to do this will, in itself, lift our mind into a more receptive attitude.

Obviously, a response like this requires a determined act of the will, but now look at the promised results, in the next verse: "And the peace of God, which transcends all understanding, will guard your hearts and your minds in Christ Jesus" (Philippians 4: 7). The peace of God will guard our hearts and minds from sinking into worry, panic or depression. As I said earlier, this course of action appears very difficult to adopt, but that is because we are approaching it purely with our mind and emotions, but God promises a peace that *"transcends all understanding"*. We can have peace when it does not make sense to have peace.

The apostle Paul, who delivered this promise, had earlier proved the truth of it in the very city to which his letter was addressed, as recorded by his friend Luke in Acts Chapter 16. Paul and Silas were preaching the good news in Philippi when they were arrested by a mob, publicly flogged, thrown into prison and fastened in stocks. The "only natural" response to that would have been bitterness and resentment, and worry about what would happen next, but instead they were singing hymns to God at midnight! They evidently had a peace and joy that transcended understanding – it just did not make sense in that situation.

I believe that it is possible to identify some practical steps to peace from the Scriptures I have quoted. The first step is to make a consistent investment in peace by depositing the promises of God in our hearts. The greater the deposit, the less perturbed we will be by any sudden threat. This is how we can have our minds "stayed" on God. The next step, when trouble does arise, is to make a conscious decision not to give way to worry or fear; "Do not let your hearts be troubled". Instead, we begin to draw on our deposit of the Word of God, and to *speak out* His love and care for us. Step three is "by prayer", in which we tell God all about the situation. This is not because He does not know about it, but our telling, *in faith*, constitutes the casting of our cares on Him. Then, as step four, comes the petition, when we ask God to meet our need, and if we are aware of a promise that relates directly to it, now is the time to *speak it back to Him*, in the confidence that He is always faithful to His Word. The final step is "with thanksgiving". However great our present need or lack, we should always be thanking God for the needs He has supplied, and the blessings He has given us so far. There is also the opportunity to take a real step of faith by thanking God for the answer to our prayer *before we see it*.

This last step does not make sense to the logical mind, but the reward is that "the peace of God, which transcends all understanding, will guard your hearts and your minds in Christ Jesus". May you know and enjoy the peace that Jesus bequeathed to you.

Key Verses

Isaiah 26: 3 You will keep him in perfect peace, whose mind is stayed on you (NKJV).

Psalm 55: 22 Cast your cares on him and he will sustain you.

Philippians 4: 6,7 Do not be anxious about anything, but in everything, by prayer and petition, with thanksgiving, present your requests to God. And the peace of God, which transcends all understanding, will guard your hearts and your minds in Christ Jesus.

Isaiah 53: 5 He was pierced for our transgressions, he was crushed for our iniquities; the punishment that brought us peace was upon him, and by his wounds we are healed.

Prayer

Father, I thank you that Jesus went to such lengths, and suffered so much, to bring me into your peace. Please help me to deposit more of your Word in my heart so that I may live in it day by day. Amen.

17 | JOY IN JESUS

I began this book on "Foundations for Joy" with a reference to some words of Jesus; after teaching His followers the importance of remaining in His love He said, "I have told you this so that my joy may be in you and that your joy may be complete" (John 15:11). This reveals His earnest desire for you and me, and it shows that He knew that a vital condition for His desire to be fulfilled is that we should "remain in His love". *The ultimate foundation for our joy is our relationship with Jesus.*

There was once an insurmountable barrier between us and His joy, namely our sin, but *He completely demolished it* when "He himself bore our sins in his body on the tree, so that we might die to sins and live for righteousness" (1 Peter 2: 24). "God made him who had no sin to be sin for us, so that *in him* we might become the righteousness of God" (2 Corinthians 5: 21). All the blessings of the Christian life are "in Him", and they become ours as we live "in Him". Paul knew this when he wrote "Praise be to the God and Father of our Lord Jesus Christ, who *has* blessed us in the heavenly realms with every spiritual blessing *in Christ*" (Ephesians 1: 3). So the way to a life of joy is wide open, and we can experience it as we "remain in His love".

The joy of which Jesus speaks is not a "bubbly feeling" (though it may give rise to some at times!). It is not even a feeling of well-being, but rather a deep underlying *knowing* of well-being which no outward circumstances can shake. If you have taken to heart the truths outlined in the previous chapters then you have the basis for this joy. In those chapters I have repeatedly emphasised the word "choose", and if we choose to believe and receive these truths then we can choose to express joy about them. In Chapter 16, I quoted from Philippians Chapter 4 where Paul says, "Do not be anxious about anything", but immediately prior to that he writes, "Rejoice in the Lord always. I will say it again: Rejoice!" (Philippians 4: 4). If God is telling us to rejoice *always* then our rejoicing is obviously not intended to depend on our feelings or circumstances. It is something that we can choose to do as we review the goodness of God and His provision for us, and as we remain in the love of Jesus.

The big question, then, is "how do we remain in Jesus and His love?" He Himself gave the answer: "If you obey my commands, you will remain in my love, just as I have obeyed my Father's commands and remain in his love" (John 15: 10). At first sight this may seem a formidable condition, but, in the previous chapter, He had given the key to the kind of obedience He was looking for: "If you love me, you will obey what I command" (John 14: 15). He was not desiring an obedience born of fear or reluctance, but one which arose naturally out of our love for Him. *Our level of obedience will be directly related to the level of our love for Him, and our love for Him will depend on the depth of our appreciation of His love for us;* "We love Him because He first loved us" (1 John 4: 19, NKJV).

This brings us back to the foundation of our joy, namely, our relationship with Jesus, and that relationship needs to be nurtured and cultivated day by day. Any human relationship thrives on affirmation and encouragement, and we can treat Jesus like that when we praise and worship Him. Worship has been defined as "admiring God and telling Him so", and we deepen our relationship with our Father and Jesus when we do that. We also enrich our bond with Him as we confide in Him about every area of our life. He already knows the details but He likes to be consulted, and He loves us so dearly that He longs to share our concerns, our interests, and our joys.

Above all, we delight Jesus when we trust Him over every aspect of our life, especially in adverse circumstances. We would certainly be encouraged if a friend entrusted us with something very important and precious to them, and likewise, we bless Jesus when we trust Him in that way. Needless to say, as His hands are the safest in the universe, we cannot fail to benefit when He takes up what we have entrusted to Him, and so our relationship grows, and so does our joy.

So I encourage you to praise Jesus every day, to discuss all your affairs with Him, to trust Him implicitly, and to live to please Him, so that you remain in His love. "Rejoice in the Lord always. I will say it again: Rejoice!" May the joy of Jesus be in you, and may your joy be complete.

Key Verses

John 15: 10 If you obey by commands, you will remain in my love, just as I have obeyed my Father's commands and remain in his love.

John 14: 15 If you love me, you will obey what I command.

John 15: 11 I have told you this so that my joy may be in you and that your joy may be complete.

Prayer

Father, when I view all the blessings that you have made available to me in Jesus, I am deeply grateful. Please help me to enter fully into His joy as I live day by day in loving obedience. Amen.

If you are a bookseller, no matter where you are in the world, and you would like to sell this book to your customers, please contact

Harvest Fields Distribution
Unit 17 Churchill Business Park
Churchill Road
DONCASTER
DN1 2TF
UK

Tel: +44 (0)1302 367868
Fax: +44 (0)1302 361006

for wholesaling details.

Obtaining your copies from this source ensures that profits from the sales go to extend God's Kingdom.